Birds through the lens of Ron Willocks

Published by Visual Impact Company of America, Inc. Boca Raton, Florida

BIRDS
THROUGH THE LENS OF
RON WILLOCKS

Text by Mrs. Henry E. Robinson, Jr.
Edited by Eddie Burgess Beitler
and Paula B. Tibbetts
Design by Lee Maxwell

Published by Visual Impact Company of America, Inc.

Contents copyrighted © 1975 by Visual Impact Company
of America, Inc. All rights reserved. No part of this book
may be reproduced, stored in a retrieval system or transmitted
in any form by a mechanical, electronic, photocopying,
recording means or otherwise without prior written permission
of the publisher. Printed in the U.S.A.

Visual Impact Company of America, Inc.
301 West Camino Gardens Boulevard
Boca Raton, Florida 33432

TABLE OF CONTENTS

Brown Pelican	4	Noddy Tern	43
Anhinga	5	Mourning Dove	44
Magnificent Frigatebird	6	Ground Dove	45
Great Blue Heron	7	Screech Owl	46
Green Heron	8	Great Horned Owl	47
Little Blue Heron	9	Burrowing Owl	48
Cattle Egret	10	Chuck-will's Widow	49
Snowy Egret	11	Common Nighthawk	50
Yellow-crowned Night Heron	12	Red-bellied Woodpecker	51
Least Bittern	13	Blue Jay	52
American Bittern	14	Scrub Jay	53
Fulvous Tree Duck	15	Long-billed Marsh Wren	54
Blue-winged Teal	16	Mockingbird	55
Lesser Scaup	17	Gray Catbird	56
Everglade Kite	18, 19	Brown Thrasher	57
Osprey	20	American Robin	58
American Kestrel	21	Loggerhead Shrike	59
Bobwhite	22	White-eyed Vireo	60
Sandhill Crane	23	Black-and-White Warbler	61
Sora	24	Tennessee Warbler	62
Purple Gallinule	25	Northern Parula	63
Common Gallinule	26	Black-throated Blue Warbler	64
American Coot	27	Prairie Warbler	65
Wilson's Plover	28, 29	Palm Warbler	66
Killdeer	30	Ovenbird	67
Ruddy Turnstone	31	Northern Water-thrush	68
Common Snipe	32	Common Yellowthroat	69
Willet	33	Yellow-breasted Chat	70
Dowitcher	34	American Redstart	71
Black-necked Stilt	35	House Sparrow	72
Ring-billed Gull	36	Spotted-breasted Oriole	73
Laughing Gull	37	Summer Tanager	74
Forster's Tern	38	Cardinal	75
Sooty Tern	39	Painted Bunting	76
Least Tern	40, 41	Cape Sable Seaside Sparrow	77
Sandwich Tern	42	Swamp Sparrow	78

BROWN PELICAN
Pelecanus occidentalis

Once plentiful, this saltwater bird, which breeds along eastern and western coasts, is now an endangered species. Persistent pesticides in its feeding waters has resulted in such life-threatening conditions as thinning or absence of an eggshell.

ANHINGA
Anhinga anhinga

The common name "snake-bird" is most suitable for the Anhinga. When hunting prey, the bird's body is submerged and its long, slender neck weaves and pumps above the waterline. It feeds and breeds in the quiet freshwater lakes and canals, swamps and marshes of the south.

MAGNIFICENT FRIGATEBIRD
Fregata magnificens

A 7½-foot wingspread and a long, deeply forked tail characterize this magnificent flier of southeastern coastal waters and occasionally the lower west coastal areas. Flocks may be seen soaring lazily at great heights, seeming to hang motionless in the sky as they search the sea for food. At times they rob other seabirds of their catches through vicious swoops and harassment.

GREAT BLUE HERON
Ardea herodias

The most widely distributed American heron, this bird is at home in any type of water as its principal food is fish. At times this stately bird feeds in drier areas on insects and small rodents. The habit of standing knee-deep in water as motionless as a statue, awaiting the unwary fish or frog, makes this 4-foot heron a skillful and patient hunter.

GREEN HERON
Butorides virescens

The smallest of the herons, with the exception of the Least Bittern, this stocky inhabitant of salt marshes, freshwater ponds, and woodland swamps and creeks, is more solitary than the larger herons and more like its other relatives — the shy bitterns. Unlike other herons, on occasion the Green Heron will dive headfirst into water for prey. Both species use their rapier-like bills for spearing food. A hunched-up posture is typical of this heron which often appears to be blue rather than green. It is quite common over the eastern half of the United States. A paler form is found in the far west.

LITTLE BLUE HERON
Florida caerulea

The young Little Blue Heron is all white! This coloring predominates into the spring of the bird's second year at which time it becomes parti-colored. It is one of comparatively few birds that mates and rears young while still in its juvenile plumage. After the breeding season it wanders far north and beyond its breeding grounds in both salt- and freshwater areas.

CATTLE EGRET
Bubulcus ibis

This African native has confounded ornithologists with its explosive spread throughout the United States since its discovery in Florida in 1941. After colonizing South America in the 1930s, it was recorded as a new bird to Australia in 1948. Although extremely beneficial, many scientists view this recent immigrant with concern since it nests in the same habitat as other native herons which are generally on the decline. Its numbers are now in the tens of thousands from coast to coast and into Canada. The Cattle Egret now is considered the most numerous heron in this country.

SNOWY EGRET
Leucophoyx thula

A full display of the delicate nuptial plumes known as aigrettes can be seen as this bird approaches the nest to greet its mate and young. The graceful, curving plumes of head, breast, and back are raised and spread like a gossamer fan. In the early 1900s the Snowy Egret was endangered when its beautiful aigrettes were used on milady's millinery. It now breeds through central and southern United States.

YELLOW-CROWNED NIGHT HERON
Nyctanassa violacea

As the name implies, this heron leaves the roost at twilight to forage in the freshwater marshes and tidal mud flats throughout the semitropical areas of the United States. It also feeds at all hours of the day. In 1840 Audubon reported that this heron was a delicacy to the Creoles of Louisiana. Its diet of crabs and crawfish with small portions of fish may account for this preference.

LEAST BITTERN
Ixobrychus exilis

As its name implies, the Least Bittern, measuring about one foot in length, is the smallest member of the heron family. One of these birds captured by Audubon was able to compress its body and pass between two books set one inch apart! Like the retiring rail and its shy relative the American Bittern, this bird prefers the freshwater ponds and reedy marshes, and the grassy margins of lakes for hunting a variety of animal life. It is fairly common in the eastern half of the United States and less common on the west coast.

AMERICAN BITTERN
Botaurus lentiginosus

Thoreau called this bird the "genius of the bog." Labeled a recluse, and adept at concealment, it stands motionless and inconspicuous among reeds and grasses. It has mastered the art of moving as slowly as the minute hand of a clock and will hide in thick brush for hours. The American Bittern can be found in freshwater marshes throughout the United States.

FULVOUS TREE DUCK
Dendrocygna bicolor

This long-legged duck exhibits many of the characteristics of geese. Its favorite foods are seeds, especially those from rice and corn fields. This bird walks and wades instead of diving and swimming. It prefers nocturnal feeding throughout its limited range and, contrary to its name, nests in grassy banks more often than in trees. It is found sporadically around lower east and Gulf coasts, and south-central California areas.

BLUE-WINGED TEAL
Anas discors

This small, fast-flying duck is found throughout the United States in smaller potholes, bayous, and lagoons. During migration it is the first to arrive at warm climes in fall and the last to depart from them in spring. Teal have an elaborate courtship and mating ritual — in the air — performing acrobatic twisting and turning which requires much agility and stamina.

LESSER SCAUP
Aythya affinis

In winter and early spring, great flotillas of Scaup may be seen just offshore in harbors, bays, and lakes along almost the entire perimeter of the United States. During migrations this abundant duck blankets the continent. It feeds by diving. A flock will settle over a mussel bed or clam flat and dive again and again until hunger is satisfied. In some localities this bird will become quite tame and may be hand fed.

EVERGLADE KITE
Rostrhamus sociabilis

This very rare bird is on the list of endangered species. Found in the United States only in Florida, its numbers fluctuate roughly between 40 and 90. These few birds roam between Lake Okeechobee and Loxahatchee National Wildlife Refuge, feeding primarily on the freshwater snail, **Pomacea paludosa**. Photographer, Ron Willocks, heads a Florida group committed to saving this unique bird.

OSPREY
Pandion haliaetus

Once common throughout the United States, the "fish hawk" is another victim of land poisons concentrated in sea life. Osprey food consists solely of live fish. A sharp decrease in numbers of osprey and eagles has been evidenced by sterile adults, infertile eggs, and abandoned nests.

AMERICAN KESTREL
Falco sparverius

Inhabiting almost the entire continent, this is the smallest and most sociable hawk. Of all the falcons, this colorful sparrow hawk is the most beneficial, consuming quantities of insects, spiders, lizards, snakes, amphibians, mice, and an occasional small bird. As the kestrel hunts, it may be seen hovering in mid-air, wings suspended, and appearing to be motionless.

BOBWHITE
Colinus virginianus

One of the favorite birds of the eastern United States, the Bobwhite is a family creature. It is thought that most quail mate for life, the male being very attentive to and protective of his mate and family. Coveys are organized for maximum protection. At night they gather in a tight circle with all tails pointing in and heads out. If threatened, the flock bursts apart and escapes in all directions. Coveys constantly "converse" with each other as they feed and wander about. The young bird responds immediately to the note of its parents, and scatters for cover until called after all danger has passed.

SANDHILL CRANE
Grus canadensis

This wary "prairie scout" from western and middle United States includes a Florida race which now is classified as "threatened." The complicated courtship dance of this handsome bird consists of solemn, low bows, spasmodic hops and skips, pirouettes, and three- and four-foot leaps into the air. Sometimes partners are facing, other times they circle together frequently uttering a wild, rolling call. This may ensue for several hours as others join the dance, continuing until all are exhausted.

SORA
Porzana carolina

This small denizen of bogs and marshes is the rail of the hunters. It is widely distributed over the North American continent. So long as its small marsh world remains intact, it has succeeded in surviving civilization even in the heart of a big city. Shy and retiring, as are most marsh dwellers, it is seldom seen except toward dusk when it may feed along the edges of its bog.

PURPLE GALLINULE
Porphyrula martinica

The Purple Gallinule has been called "the most photographed bird in Florida." Surely, it is one of the most colorful. It shares the same habitat and characteristics as its cousin, the Common Gallinule, but it is much shier and its diet contains more animal matter. When nest building, it prefers areas where the wampee plant and pickerelweed are plentiful. Several dummy nests may be constructed, perhaps attempts to confuse its many predators. The Gallinule's unusually long, bright yellow toes are spread wide, offering good support as it walks on lily pads. This freshwater marsh bird has a very restricted range around the Gulf and lower east coasts.

COMMON GALLINULE
Gallinula chloropus

Here is another elusive, hen-like bird of the freshwater marshes and ponds which prefers to walk and swim rather than fly. Gallinules have an extensive repertoire of harsh calls and chatterings. Should a mated pair become separated, the two constantly call to each other. The Gallinule is common throughout the eastern half of the United States and along the California coast.

AMERICAN COOT
Fulica americana

This "clown of the pond" is a member of the rail family. Probably the most abundant waterfowl in the United States, the coot is a noisy and active inhabitant of ponds, lakes, and marshes, as well as of saltwater bays. This entertaining "water hen" is most vocal, uttering toots and grunts and cries. It dives and skitters over the water with much splashing and spattering, giving rise to such common names as: "flusterer," "shuffler," and "pull-doo."

WILSON'S PLOVER
Charadrius wilsonia

Along the most southern beaches of the United States, from east to west, this stout-billed plover is an uncommon bird. Its scooped-out nest is found on dry beaches where bits of shells and ocean debris camouflage the speckled eggs, usually at the base of a clump of grass or other light shelter. The female plover could vie for an Academy Award for her fearless performance near the nest, decoying intruders with what appears to be a broken wing or lame leg, and general disability, as she skillfully struggles along the sands, luring the predator farther and farther from the nest, her mate piping alarm and support overhead. Satisfied with the distance and distraction, she springs into the air, circles off, and returns to the nest when all is safe.

KILLDEER
Charadrius vociferus

This abundant plover has earned its species name, "vociferus," by frequently repeating the sound, "kill-dee-dee." During courtship it flies back and forth over a field for more than an hour, calling its own name. Ascending into the sky with its mate, it performs aerial acrobatics and utters call notes. Ground displays are accompanied by trilling notes. This most common of the banded plovers is also a most beneficial bird, eating great quantities of harmful insects. It frequents borders of lakes, seas, meadows, and pastures throughout the continent.

RUDDY TURNSTONE
Arenaria interpres

Shorebirds, as a class, are foremost among earth's greatest travelers, many breeding along arctic shores and wintering in South America. One hundred years ago massed legions of shorebirds, comprising many species, wheeled and dipped over prairies, salt marshes, mud flats, and seashores. Now, vast areas are empty and silent due to the relentless and wanton slaughter of past years. Turnstones hanging in Boston markets were 10 cents a dozen! Killdeer almost disappeared. Once again turnstones are appearing along the seashore, turning over stones, shells, eating eggs of crabs, worms, mussels, and marine flotsam.

COMMON SNIPE
Capella gallinago

Authorities say this long-billed marsh recluse, covering the entire continent, was the most heavily shot game bird in the history of North American field sport. Three hundred sixty-six snipe were shot in 6 hours by one hunter in 1877! This same hunter tallied his twenty-year kill of snipe at 69,087! A succulent table bird, it hung in the big city market stalls by the thousands. Today, only a remnant remains of the myriad of shorebirds which once graced this continent.

WILLET
Catoptrophorus semipalmatus

During the nesting season this large wader frantically patrols and protects his family by flying around constantly screaming and crying his several calls. The striking black-and-white wing pattern seems to ward off all intruders. The Willet breeds along the coast of the eastern United States and on lakes in its western range.

DOWITCHER
Limnodromus griseus

The Long-billed and Short-billed Dowitchers, among the least wary of all North American shorebirds, missed by a hair's breadth joining the "legion of the vanished." For years, the guns of market hunters raked flocks of these unsuspicious and gentle birds through spring, summer, and fall, setting a record of slaughter, not by the hundreds but by brimming wagonloads. Audubon saw 127 killed at once by the discharge of three barrels! A hundred years ago, shorebird flights deserved a place among the truly great wildlife spectacles of this continent.

BLACK-NECKED STILT
Himantopus mexicanus

This striking, long-legged wader is another of the birds brought to the verge of extinction years ago by indiscriminate shooting. No chapter in the long history of North American wildlife is more shameful than that of shorebird killings. Found occasionally along southern coasts, the stilt occurs more commonly along the southwestern coast and inland.

RING-BILLED GULL
Larus delawarensis

The gull family is one of the most interesting in the bird world. Scientists are reluctant to assign "intelligence" to members of the avian group, but this extraordinary family exhibits what could be called "thinking." Gulls show great adaptability and will drop clams and crabs on hard surfaces to break the shells. Mostly monogamous, they recognize their own mates even after months of traveling widely over land and sea. A rigid social order exists in the colonies, with the older gulls ranking highest. Young gulls must keep their necks pulled in to show their low status! The Ring-billed Gull ranges over the continent.

LAUGHING GULL
Larus atricilla

Masters of marathon flights, spending most of their day over coastal waters from Nova Scotia around the Gulf to southeastern California, gulls have their own unique, built-in desalination device. Glands above the eyes excrete salt through small openings in the upper mandible. This gull's food consists primarily of small fish and other sea creatures. It is not a scavenger like the larger gulls. Plume hunters almost exterminated the large colonies of this "merry" gull at the turn of the century.

FORSTER'S TERN
Sterna forsteri

Called "sea-swallows," all terns are graceful and expert fliers. A characteristic of terns which distinguishes them from their close relatives, the gulls, is the constant "looking-up-and-down" head movement when hunting fish. Most terns hover and then dive headfirst into water after their prey; gulls do not. The Forster's was not recognized at first as being a different species from its close cousin the Common Tern. But the Forster's likes marshy as well as coastal areas, and therefore has a more varied diet. This tern is common over almost all of the United States.

SOOTY TERN
Sterna fuscata

The Sooty is sometimes called the "wide-awake" bird because of the constant screaming, day and night, in its breeding colonies. On the Islands of the Tortugas off the Florida Keys, colonies of Sootys and Noddys are banded regularly to gather further information on the life histories of these ocean birds. Returns from these bandings indicate that some of these seabirds live for at least thirty years! The Sooty is an abundant inhabitant of tropical and subtropical seas, coasts, and islands.

LEAST TERN
Sterna albifrons

The smallest of the terns is trying desperately to adapt to man's environment. It was once plentiful along the open sandy beaches of the east and Gulf coasts and the bare, inland sandbars. Today, it also is found nesting on flat rooftops of large buildings where the hatchlings have been drowned during periods of heavy rain. Other nesting places are fill banks from newly dredged canals and areas of crushed limestone in campgrounds. This tern became nearly extinct years ago when as many as 1400 were killed in one day for their delicate plumage. The millinery trade bought them for 10 cents apiece!

SANDWICH TERN
Thalasseus sandvicensis

From its limited range in the extreme southeastern and Gulf waters, this skillful flier appears to be extending its range northward and increasing in number. Usually it is found nesting and feeding in association with another crested cousin, the Royal Tern. The Sandwich Tern often will dive beneath the surface of the water in pursuit of prey, and is undaunted in hunting, even in stormy weather. It is believed that these lovely terns mate for life and, unlike other terns, share equally in the incubation of their eggs.

NODDY TERN
Anous stolidus

As its name suggests, this beautiful dusky tern of the tropical Tortugas does much bowing and nodding to its mate as well as to any strange Noddy alighting nearby. This is the only North American tern that utilizes small bushes, shrubs, sticks, seaweed, and other similar material for nesting off the ground, although some do build nests on sand as do most other terns. Usually, only one egg is laid.

MOURNING DOVE
Zenaidura macroura

About 25 years ago ornithologists began observing an interesting development in the movement of the much-hunted Mourning Dove. This common bird of open fields throughout the continent, now is moving in greater and greater numbers into the protection of cities. It appears to be discovering "natural sanctuaries" such as cattle ranches as well as backyard feeders. Such adaptability could mean that this hunter's delight will be one of the few feathered creatures to survive the crush of man.

GROUND DOVE
Columbigallina passerina

This smallest of North American doves is appropriately named. Usually found in pairs, this bird walks along the ground constantly hunting for seeds, grain, and insects. If flushed, this unwary cousin of the pigeon flies up a few inches, then alights a short distance ahead and continues the hunt for food. Because it eats large quantities of noxious weed seeds, it is a most beneficial bird. The Ground Dove is found mostly in the extreme southern portions of the United States from east to west coasts.

SCREECH OWL
Otus asio

There is a superstition in parts of the deep south, that should one hear the quavering call of the little Screech Owl, a death in the family is imminent and only immediate action can halt the tragedy. The antidote is to hold tightly to the iron rim of the bedspring until the iron is hot in the hand. This heat is said to burn the owl's feet, forcing him to fly away, thus breaking the spell! There are other fascinating remedies for the imagined evil this North American "feathered wildcat" portends.

GREAT HORNED OWL
Bubo virginianus

Writings on this "winged tiger" comprise all the superlatives ever applied to a bird: fearless, powerful, aggressive, courageous, overpowering, magnificent bearing, untamable ferocity, extremely beneficial. Apparently, all are true when applied to this noiseless, mostly nocturnal hunter of anything that moves. Along with the small mammals, insects, birds, reptiles, and amphibians, its prey includes skunks and porcupines — quills and all! There is an extraordinary report of an attack on a fencing mask worn by a man near a nest. The powerful talons penetrated it and the man's scalp! **Bubo,** its latin name, is translated as "eagle owl," although the 4-foot wingspread is several feet less than that of its namesake. The Great Horned Owl ranges over most of the North American continent.

BURROWING OWL
Speotyto cunicularia

This long-legged, small owl of open ranges, prairies, sand traps on golf courses, airports, and grassy areas, inhabits the western United States and a few south Florida sites. It is not as plentiful in the west as it was once because the prairie dog, whose deserted burrow it adopts, is now considered a farmland pest and is being "chemically controlled." The long burrow is irregularly shaped, extends into the sand from five to ten feet, and is used year after year. This owl, primarily an insect eater, has been observed following larger animals in open fields, presumably watching for insects somewhat in the manner of the Cattle Egret.

Photograph by R. Nick Willocks

CHUCK-WILL'S WIDOW
Caprimulgus carolinensis

The overlapping range of this nocturnal species with the Whip-poor-will results in a confusion of names. They sometimes are used interchangeably. To differentiate between the calls, the Whip-poor-will repeats its three-syllable name in closer sequence, and usually for longer duration. Almost complete camouflage is brought to perfection in these two lookalikes. When resting lengthwise on a limb, it is almost impossible to differentiate between this bird and a knot on the tree. The Chuck breeds in the eastern half of the United States, but not in the more northern areas.

COMMON NIGHTHAWK
Chordeiles minor

Commonly called "bull bat," the rapid, erratic flight of the Nighthawk is quite similar to other avian aerialists — the swallow, and the bat. Its huge mouth, the gape extending back under the ear, is a perfect trap for catching all types of flying insects. This wide yawn is also employed as a threat when approached at its nest. If this fails to frighten the enemy, it will perform the convincing wounded-bird act. The Nighthawk is a ground and flat-roof nester over most of the North American continent.

RED-BELLIED WOODPECKER
Centurus carolinus

Too often the Red-bellied Woodpecker is confused with its cousin, the Red-headed Woodpecker, since both have types of red heads. The Red-headed has a hood of red covering the entire head — top, back, sides, and throat. The red on the head of the Red-bellied is confined to forehead, crown, and nape of neck — like a natural hairline. The name, Red-bellied, is derived from a tinge of red on the abdomen, which is very difficult to see when the bird is in its typical vertical position. The Red-bellied Woodpecker is a common breeder in most of the eastern United States. The Red-headed is uncommon throughout the Red-bellied Woodpecker's range.

BLUE JAY
Cyanocitta cristata

In order to appreciate and accept the Blue Jay, it is important to remember that it is a member of the crow family. Thus, some of the less admirable characteristics, such as nest-robbing and occasional predation, may be understood better. However, the good qualities outweigh the bad habits. Where there are acorns, the Jay — like the squirrel — sets about burying the surplus for winter reserves. In time many sprout, and the process of reforestation begins. Other wild things take cover when the ever-alert Jay shrieks the "jay, jay, jay" call at the intrusion of man into the forest, or when it spies a snake, cat, hawk, owl, or other predator. The Blue Jay uses this same call as a ploy to vacate the feeding tray! This unique bird is resourceful, handsome, active, courageous, and mischievous — while most interesting to observe. It is common over more than half of the eastern United States.

SCRUB JAY
Aphelocoma coerulescens

It is hard to believe this gentle bird is also a member of the crow family. This trusting jay will alight on the hand to take bread, raisins, nuts, or other tidbits. On occasion it can be stroked while on the nest. It is almost rare occurring locally in scrub areas of Florida exclusively. In south Florida its survival is threatened by the extensive clearing of its habitat for building. Another race of the Scrub Jay inhabitats a large area in the western United States and is considered common.

LONG-BILLED MARSH WREN
Telmatodytes palustris

Wrens are noted for their insatiable curiosity. They investigate everything and anything. No bird is as indefatigable a forager of insects and spiders as is the wren. In its activities it is quick to spot and announce to the world by means of insect-like sounds the discovery of a predator or intruder. Wren songs are considered to be among the best in the bird world but not the song of this "imp of the marshes." It will sing not only during the day but also at night. It builds several dummy nests before settling on one which it lines with cattail down. The Marsh Wren is found in salt- and freshwater marshes over most of the United States.

MOCKINGBIRD
Mimus polyglottos

Mimus polyglottos translates as "many-tongued mimic." In strictest musical terms the Mockingbird's song is a rhapsody — irregular in form and full of improvisation. It is possible to identify area birds by listening carefully to the song of an adult bird. The young sing as vigorously, but have yet to learn what to mimic. In this age of the cassette recorder, many backyard birders are finding a new interest by recording this truly remarkable and accommodating singer. The Mockingbird is found throughout the lower half of the United States, but is steadily extending its range northward.

GRAY CATBIRD
Dumetella carolinensis

A close cousin of the Mockingbird, this mimic thrush can and does mimic but seems to prefer its own inventions peppered with the squeaks and squawks so typical of this species. A petulant whine or mewing note is the catcall from which it gets its name. It is a very attentive and devoted parent. There are reports that catbirds have cared for orphaned young of other species. The range of the catbird does not extend quite to the west coast but does encompass the remainder of the United States.

BROWN THRASHER
Toxostoma rufum

This is another mimic thrush often called Wood Thrush, and sometimes mistaken for that species. It has been suggested that this bird's surname derives from its constant pitching and tossing of leaves in all directions as it hunts for food. A strong bill is used for thrashing large insects on the ground or limb and preparing them for eating or feeding to its young. While not as accomplished a mimic as the mocker, the Thrasher produces a quality of song equally beautiful. The clue to this song, most often given from the top of a tall tree, is the constant repetition of each phrase, sometimes repeated in 3s, rarely 4s. The Brown Thrasher is a common bird in rural and urban areas over the greater half of the United States.

AMERICAN ROBIN
Turdus migratorius

Surely no other bird is as beloved as the American Robin, the largest of the true thrushes of which the Bluebird and Wood Thrush are species. Its namesake is the European Robin, a distant cousin. Early settlers noting the similarity, named this bird. It is difficult to believe that in Audubon's day these gentle birds were slaughtered by the bagful and sold as a table delicacy. The robin is one of few birds that will not allow the egg of the parasitic cowbird to remain in its nest. Robins are common over all of the North American continent.

LOGGERHEAD SHRIKE
Lanius ludovicianus

It is difficult to balance the good and bad in this so-called "butcher bird." The Loggerhead Shrike has several characteristics in common with predatory hawks and owls. It pursues prey with much flying skill and has a decidedly hooked, sharp bill for tearing it. It also is an early nester, as are other birds of prey. This bird disgorges pellets containing indigestible parts of victims, as do the hawks and owls. But its value to agriculture far outweighs this predatory way of life. Primarily an insect eater, it consumes great quantities of grasshoppers and other destructive insects as well as rats and mice. The Loggerhead Shrike is not as common throughout the United States as it once was, partly because of the increased use of insecticides on farmlands and roadsides which it frequents.

WHITE-EYED VIREO
Vireo griseus

When first observing the behavior of tree birds it is difficult to separate the vireos from the warblers. But with patience and persistence the observer begins to notice that the vireo is much more deliberate in movement and not in such a hurry as is the warbler. The bill is slightly heavier and is almost imperceptibly hooked. Vireos and warblers are our most beneficial vacuum cleaners of forest trees and shrubs. They are almost exclusively insect eaters, but they do enjoy small berries and fruits. The song of the White-eyed Vireo is completely different from any other vireo and may be heard almost the year around. Vireos are heavily parasitized by cowbirds. The White-eyed is a common bird of the southeastern United States.

BLACK-AND-WHITE WARBLER
Mniotilta varia

A greater toll of warblers is taken at the TV tower kills than any other bird. Most warblers are night migrants and any tall obstruction with a height of about 500 feet or more, is a hazard. Tall buildings which are lighted for decorative purposes, lighthouses, TV towers, the guy wires steadying the towers, and airport ceilometer lights, are death traps for migrants, especially in inclement weather. Untold thousands are killed during each spring and fall migration. At one TV tower in west Florida, 417 Black-and-White Warblers were killed during an eleven year study. The heaviest casualties occur in the fall when great numbers of young birds are making their first migration. The Black-and-White Warbler is a striking bark-creeper, common over more than half of the eastern United States and Canada.

TENNESSEE WARBLER
Vermivora peregrina

North American Wood Warblers are a family known as the **Parulidae** with more than 100 species essentially restricted to the New World. They are colorful and varied with yellow as the dominant color. In most migratory species, such as the Tennessee Warbler, the adult plumage of the female differs considerably from that of the adult male. But among the non-migratory species both male and female are quite similar. The Tennessee Warbler is a difficult warbler to identify. It can be confused easily with several of the vireos as well as several of its own family. It breeds throughout Canadian forests and the extreme northeastern United States, and migrates through central and eastern U.S. to Central America.

NORTHERN PARULA
Parula americana

Warbler songs vary in pitch, volume, and quality and may differ considerably not only among the species but also among individuals of the same species. As a group they are not considered outstanding vocalists. Most of the songs are high pitched. They can be weak or loud, buzzing or trilling, and occasionally musical. The tiny parula has a buzzy song which it voices not only during nesting season but also infrequently during the winter season. It has a decided preference for urban and suburban areas which contain the tree lichen **Usnea**, or the more southern airplant **Tillandsia** (Spanish moss). It is common throughout the eastern half of the United States and Canadian borders. The mortality rate of this lovely bird at TV kills is high. During the aforementioned eleven-year study in west Florida more than 1,227 were killed.

BLACK-THROATED BLUE WARBLER
Dendroica caerulescens

Warblers are extremely beneficial. They are tireless in their search for insects of all kinds and in all stages — in the foliage and trunks of trees, around the buds of trees and shrubs, on aquatic reeds and grasses, brushy areas of fields, and on the ground wherever insects may hide. A minor food consists of several varieties of small berries. The Black-throated Blue is a common warbler in evergreen forests in the eastern portion of the United States and along the Canadian border.

PRAIRIE WARBLER
Dendroica discolor

When migrating across the Gulf, birds are fortunate to have as either their last or first port of call, the Dry Tortugas, an isolated group of islands surrounded by water, sixty miles west of Key West, Florida. This is not only a nesting area for Noddy and Sooty Terns but a welcome landfall for trans-Gulf migrants. At Ft. Jefferson, located on one of those islands, the Tropical Audubon Society of Miami installed a freshwater fountain just for the birds! The Prairie Warbler rests and drinks at that fountain. A common and beautiful yellow warbler, the Prairie is not found on the prairies but rather in low vegetation adjacent to an open area and in scrubby growth extending northward from the southeastern United States.

PALM WARBLER
Dendroica palmarum

Probably the most common warbler wintering in Florida, the Palm is a very plain and nondescript bird. It has a habit of flipping its tail as it hops about lawns and low bushes consuming many noxious insects and weed seeds. Like the parula, the palm prefers to use moss or sphagnum for its nest on the ground. This bird is a fairly common warbler, nesting primarily in boggy areas of Canada and extreme northeastern United States. It is one of the most numerous casualties at TV towers. The eleven year total at a west Florida tower was 1,861 Palm Warblers killed in migration.

OVENBIRD
Seiurus aurocapillus

This dignified ground warbler is not typical of the family, being more thrush-like in habit as well as appearance. Its name is derived from its oven-like nest with an opening on one side, usually placed at the base of a tree. As it walks sedately about the forest floor and around the garden, it searches for insects under leaves and logs. The female frequently will resort to the broken-wing act to distract a nest predator or intruder. Its nest is heavily parasitized by the cowbird. The Ovenbird is common over more than half the continent.

NORTHERN WATER-THRUSH
Seiurus noveboracensis

Another ground warbler and thrush-like bird, the water-thrush teeters along the ground in suburban gardens as well as in swamps, wooded streams, and other damp areas. Walking warblers are not common, and only two, this species and the Louisiana Water-thrush bob their bodies as they walk looking for insects. A favorite and common bird of the northern parts of the United States and into Canada, it winters mainly in south Florida, Mexico, and into South America.

COMMON YELLOWTHROAT
Geothlypis trichas

This vivacious little black-masked warbler spends much time in the lower shrubbery, thickets, and fields of a variety of habitats. It seems to prefer damp places, but also may be found in drier situations. The female lacks the black mask and is often confused with other plain warblers. The yellowthroat has a lovely, clear repetitive song which is more musical than that of most warblers. There are many subspecies in this group and they range abundantly over the continent.

YELLOW-BREASTED CHAT
Icteria virens

The chat has been called a buffoon, a clown, and a comedian. Its song is described as a collection of gurgles, squawks, mews, whistles, squeals, and other indescribable sounds — it is also something of a ventriloquist. Exhibiting unwarblerlike behavior, the chat flies about with dangling legs, wings hanging loose, and much tail pumping. This almost appears to be a performance put on especially for the observer. The chat consumes quantities of all kinds of insects and quite a variety of berries. The largest of the warblers, it is found over most of the United States.

AMERICAN REDSTART
Setophaga ruticilla

Weighing only a few grams, the redstart refreshes itself at the Ft. Jefferson water fountain. Some warblers habitually catch insects on the wing. The redstart is expert at this and has well-developed bristles at the sides of the bill which help entrap the flying insect. As it darts about, the tail is fanned out displaying a brilliant orange-and-black pattern. It is this characteristic which gives it the name of "butterfly bird," and in Latin America, "candelita," or little torch. A common, active, and vivacious warbler, it is found over all but the extreme western United States and in southern areas of Canada.

HOUSE SPARROW
Passer domesticus

In 1850 eight pair of this weaver finch were introduced in the New York area from England. They are now among the most abundant birds in the United States. Not the most desirable bird, the House Sparrow is quite noisy in large roosting flocks. Furthermore, it competes with many native birds for nesting sites. However, it is difficult not to admire the industrious behavior and adaptive qualities of this bird. The writer has observed a female sparrow gathering moths from under a sidewalk lamp late at night, in order to feed her brood which was calling from a nest over the door of a nearby building.

SPOTTED-BREASTED ORIOLE
Icterus pectoralis

The colorful orioles are members of the blackbird family which also includes bobolinks, meadowlarks, grackles, and cowbirds. This particular oriole is a stunning Central American addition to the birdlife of southeast Florida where it was discovered first in 1949. Slowly expanding its range northward within the state, it appears to roam widely in search of flowers which produce the preferred nectar. A pair will work over a large shrub or vine piercing the base of each and every flower and occasionally giving one clear whistled note as a means of communication. Orioles are noted for their rich and melodious songs as well as their striking beauty. The Spotted-breasted Oriole is abundantly endowed with both.

SUMMER TANAGER
Piranga rubra

Of the four American tanagers, this one inhabits the southern half of the United States. This summer redbird is related to the finches and prefers a rather solitary existence hiding in treetops searching for insects and fruit. Its song is rich and varied and more musical than songs of the other three tanagers. The female of this group is an olive-yellow color which serves as a camouflage in the sunlight and shadows of the leaves. This bird was photographed at the fountain at Ft. Jefferson on the Tortugas during a spring migration.

Photograph by Sherri Willocks

CARDINAL
Richmondena cardinalis

The seedeaters — grosbeaks, finches, sparrows, and buntings — are the largest family of songbirds. The heavy cone-shaped bill is particularly adapted to the crushing of seeds, which are its preferred food. Seven states have chosen the Cardinal as state bird. Obviously, its colorful beauty makes it a favorite garden resident. At one time the Cardinal was typically a southern species, but its range now is extending northward, primarily in the eastern half of the United States.

PAINTED BUNTING
Passerina ciris

Years ago this multicolored beauty was a favorite cage bird. It was called "nonpareil," which means "without equal." Considered the most colorful American songbird, it is possibly the lure which recruits more bird watchers, than any other small bird. The glossy plumage of reds, greens, violets, and blues is strangely difficult to locate when this shy bird darts from low thickets up into the shade trees. It is fairly common along the southern edges of the United States.

CAPE SABLE SEASIDE SPARROW
Ammospiza mirabilis

There are seven races of seaside sparrow, all of them very secretive and difficult to flush for observation. In degree, the Cape Sable is considered the most timid. It spends most of its time on or near the ground searching for insects and small marsh life in the fresh and brackish water saw-grass habitat. Two races of seaside sparrow are on the endangered list — this race, found only in a very restricted area a few miles inland near Cape Sable, Florida, and the Dusky Seaside Sparrow, found in the salt marshes near Cape Kennedy, Florida, plus a few isolated areas along the St. Johns River in Florida.

SWAMP SPARROW
Melospiza georgiana

William Bartram called this dark, shy sparrow of the dense bogs and cattail marshes, the "reed sparrow." It slips in and about dense tangles of reeds and grasses like a small brown mouse! If one is willing to don long rubber boots and wade into the watery, muddy places, it is possible to get a brief glimpse of this elusive sparrow. Naturally, its food consists primarily of aquatic insects, but seeds from the plants in its habitat also are eaten. Occasionally, this sparrow may be found in moist fields of dense briars. It is common over the eastern half of the continent.

INDEX

Anhinga	5
American Bittern	14
American Coot	27
American Kestrel	21
American Redstart Warbler	71
American Robin	58
Bittern, American	14
Bittern, Least	13
Black-and-White Warbler	61
Black-necked Stilt	35
Black-throated Blue Warbler	64
Blue Jay	52
Blue-winged Teal Duck	16
Bobwhite	22
Brown Pelican	4
Brown Thrasher	57
Bunting, Painted	76
Burrowing Owl	48
Cape Sable Seaside Sparrow	77
Cardinal	75
Catbird, Gray	56
Cattle Egret	10
Chat, Warbler, Yellow-breasted	70
Chuck-will's Widow	49
Common Gallinule	26
Common Nighthawk	50
Common Snipe	32
Common Yellowthroat Warbler	69
Coot, American	27
Crane, Sandhill	23
Dove, Ground	45
Dove, Mourning	44
Dowitcher	34
Duck, Blue-winged Teal	16
Duck, Fulvous Tree	15
Duck, Lesser Scaup	17
Egret, Cattle	10
Egret, Snowy	11
Everglade Kite	18, 19
Forster's Tern	38
Frigatebird, Magnificent	6
Fulvous Tree Duck	15
Gallinule, Common	26
Gallinule, Purple	25
Gray Catbird	56
Great Blue Heron	7
Great Horned Owl	47
Green Heron	8
Ground Dove	45
Gull, Laughing	37
Gull, Ring-billed	36
Heron, Great Blue	7
Heron, Green	8
Heron, Little Blue	9
Heron, Yellow-crowned Night	12
House Sparrow	72
Jay, Blue	52
Jay, Scrub	53
Kestrel, American	21
Killdeer	30
Kite, Everglade	18, 19
Laughing Gull	37
Least Bittern	13
Least Tern	40, 41
Lesser Scaup Duck	17
Little Blue Heron	9
Loggerhead Shrike	59
Long-billed Marsh Wren	54
Magnificent Frigatebird	6
Mockingbird	55
Mourning Dove	44
Nighthawk, Common	50
Noddy Tern	43
Northern Parula Warbler	63
Northern Water-thrush Warbler	68
Oriole, Spotted-breasted	73
Osprey	20
Ovenbird Warbler	67
Owl, Burrowing	48
Owl, Great Horned	47
Owl, Screech	46

Painted Bunting 76
Palm Warbler 66
Parula, Warbler, Northern 63
Pelican, Brown 4
Plover, Wilson's 28, 29
Prairie Warbler 65
Purple Gallinule 25

Red-bellied Woodpecker 51
Redstart Warbler, American 71
Ring-billed Gull 36
Robin, American 58
Ruddy Turnstone 31

Sandhill Crane 23
Sandwich Tern 42
Screech Owl 46
Scrub Jay 53
Shrike, Loggerhead 59
Snipe, Common 32
Snowy Egret 11
Sooty Tern 39
Sora 24
Sparrow, Cape Sable Seaside 77
Sparrow, House 72
Sparrow, Swamp 78
Spotted-breasted Oriole 73
Stilt, Black-necked 35
Summer Tanager 74
Swamp Sparrow 78

Tanager, Summer 74
Tennessee Warbler 62
Tern, Forster's 38
Tern, Least 40, 41
Tern, Noddy 43
Tern, Sandwich 42
Tern, Sooty 39
Thrasher, Brown 57
Turnstone, Ruddy 31

Vireo, White-eyed 60

Water-thrush Warbler, Northern 68
Warbler, Black-and-White 61
Warbler, Black-throated Blue 64

Warbler, Chat, Yellow-breasted 70
Warbler, Ovenbird 67
Warbler, Palm 66
Warbler, Parula, Northern 63
Warbler, Prairie 65
Warbler, Redstart, American 71
Warbler, Tennessee 62
Warbler, Yellow-throat, Common 69
Warbler, Water-thrush, Northern 68
White-eyed Vireo 60
Willet 33
Wilson's Plover 28, 29
Woodpecker, Red-bellied 51
Wren, Long-billed Marsh 54

Yellow-breasted Chat Warbler 70
Yellow-crowned Night Heron 12
Yellowthroat Warbler, Common 69